For my brother who always asked why
and my mom who always looked to the *Stars*.
-L.B.

ISLAND HERITAGE®
175 Kahelu Avenue
Mililani, Hawai`i 96789
Orders: (800) 468-2800
Information: (808) 564-8800
Fax: (808) 564-8877
welcometotheislands.com
COP 193005

ISBN: 1-61710-409-4
First Edition, First Printing—2019

FOREVER Mine

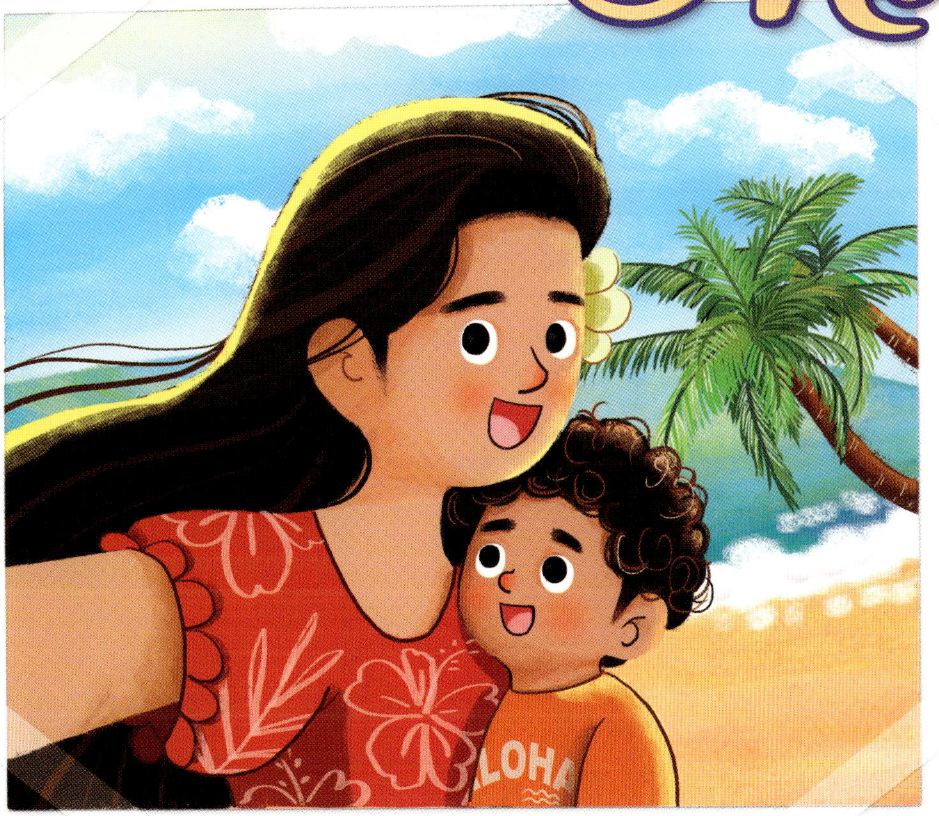

Written by Leeana Batungbacal

Illustrated by Alex Nguyen

One day
you asked,
"WHY ME?"

And I said, "WHAT *do you* MEAN?"

"Out of ALL the keiki in the World,
WHY did you choose ME?"
ALOHA

ALOH

I smiled and said,

"I LOOKED UP *at the sky* one night and saw something."

"What did you SEE?" you asked.

"A SKY FULL OF Stars."

"STARS?"

"*Yes*, stars."

"I reached up and *Pulled* ONE DOWN. THAT STAR was *You*."

"Me!"

"Yes, YOU."

"Out of all the stars
in the sky I CHOSE YOU."

"I knew
one day you
would GROW,

you would *shine,*

And you would be
Forever Mine."

The
END.